I0137376

Living the Thankful Life
Robert B. Walker

Living the Thankful Life

Visit our web site at **www.sportsspectrum.com**
Copyright © 2011 by Robert B. Walker

Page & Layout Designer Kathryn Vance
Graphic Editor Renata Bolden
Edited by Krystil Wade

All rights reserved. No portion of this book may
be reproduced, stored in a retrieval system, or
transmitted in any form or by any means –
electronic, mechanical, recording, scanning,
or other except for brief quotation in printed
reviews, without the prior permission of the publisher.

The Core Media Group Inc.
P.O. Box 2037
Indian Trail, NC 28079

Bible quotations, unless otherwise noted, are taken from
the HOLY BIBLE, NEW INTERNATIONAL VERSION.

Table of Contents

*To all the people that have impacted
my life and taught me the true
meaning of Thankfulness.*

Acknowledgements

To all of my current and former staff at Unlimited Success Sports Management and Sports Spectrum magazine. Thank you Sharon Wade, Renata Bolden, Lindsay Adams, Ryan DiNunzio, Brett Honeycutt, Brian Payne, Aaron May, Greg Arnold, Nathan Wade, Krystil Wade, Natalie Topper, Ryan DeFaber and Kathryn Vance. Thank you all for helping me to keep life simple and organized.

To my parents, Doug and Louise Walker. Thank you both for teaching me so many simple principles of life including the one I have written about, "Thankfulness."

To my wife, Jacqueline, and my kids, Hannah and Matthew. Thank you for helping support me in all I do.

There are so many more who have come alongside of me to help in so many ways; you know who you are and what you have done for me along the way, and I am thankful for your help and encouragement.

PROLOGUE:

One night while I was putting my son Matthew to bed, he said to me, "I love my blanket so much Dad! It's so comfy!" My reply was, "Well then, we need to thank the Lord for your blanket." At that instant I was convicted. I realized that we, as a society, are not always thankful for the little things we have, like a warm blanket to sleep under. We crave things to make us feel better, all the while missing the wonderful blessings God has already given us. A few days later I awoke in the middle of the night with an idea: not just for a good book about thankfulness, but with a vision for a thankful movement across the nation.

In the beginning of each chapter are short stories about my life and why I am so thankful for certain people, places, and experiences. My prayer is that these stories will inspire, encourage, and challenge you to examine your own life and all you have to be thankful for. I believe it is important to share our life stories so that we may influence others in a positive way; which is why I have given you the opportunity to write your story at the end of each chapter. One day it may be a piece your children and/or grandchildren come to treasure.

Again, this book is just the beginning of what I hope will be a nationwide movement to become a thankful society. It's just the launching ground for your family, Sunday School, Bible study, or church to get started. Consider using this book as a church-wide Bible study or as a devotional that you and your family do together. At the end of the study, you could have a "thank you celebration" by hosting a party thanking God for His goodness and mercy!

At some point during your study on thankfulness, please use the five note cards in the back to thank those who have impacted your life. You sometimes never know how much the two words "thank you" can mean to someone. "A word aptly spoken is like apples of gold in settings of silver" (Proverbs 25:11).

Sharing your thankfulness is important and can certainly become contagious. Consider sharing this book with someone that may be experiencing a difficult time and could benefit from reflecting on all the good things in his or her life.

"Praise the Lord, how good and fitting it is to praise Him" (Psalm 147:1). Praise the Lord for the great things He has done!

(place your Family photo here)

FAMILY

"Only be careful, and watch yourselves closely so that you do not forget the things your eyes have seen or let them slip from your heart as long as you live. Teach them to your children and to their children after them."
- Deuteronomy 4:9

Growing up in a family of six, there was never a dull moment. We had loads of fun throughout my childhood. My brothers and I played on many of the same athletic teams, and my dad coached us. I remember my mother always getting up very early to make breakfast or to start cooking Sunday dinner for all of us. We only had one bathroom and three bedrooms, yet I never felt like I was missing anything. My brothers and I would ride our bikes all over the neighborhood and spend a lot of time riding skateboards down "the big hill." There was even a picture of us riding down the hill in the local newspaper! Another thing we liked to do was call sports talk radio shows and ask questions about sports. We were always busy and always a family.

Our telephone time was limited, and we only had one TV in the house. This meant we often had to find other ways to amuse ourselves. Curfew was always 11:00 pm (maybe 11:30 if it was your graduation night). We went to church every Sunday morning, Sunday night, and Wednesday night. We went to Vacation Bible School (my mother was the director), Sunday School, revivals, and New Year's Eve services. Many times the neighborhood kids would gather at our house to play. We shot basketball with my mom and dad and played football (my dad was always quarter-back for both teams). We had wrestling matches, took music lessons, went fishing and played with our dog and cats. When I look back at my childhood, I realize that some people may think a lot was missing because we did not have very many material things.

But we had family: a true caring mother and father who supported and encouraged their four boys, and we all loved and respected them. As I write about family, I am reminded of how thankful I am to have had a close family and for the times we shared along life's journey. Love is not always easy. Family teaches us how to love and live with one another. We don't always realize how much we have. We compare ourselves to other people and their families and inevitably find one that appears "better" than ours. But hopefully, as you look back on your family life, you will see a unique kind of love for which you can truly be thankful.

Author's Thankful Thoughts

Still, I am sure that some reading this book
have not had ideal family situations. For you,
the stories I tell with a smile may remind you of
hurt or bring about a sense of longing for a family
bond you never experienced. Let me tell you that
God's desire is for us to be thankful in whatever
situation He's placed us. Paul said in Philippians
4:11 that he had learned to be content whatever the
circumstances in good times and bad. Even if you
find it hard to be grateful for your family (or lack
of one), remember that God put you there for a
purpose, and be thankful to Him because of all
you can learn from that situation.

Go Deeper: Ephesians 5:22-33, Ephesians 6:1-4

Points to consider as we thank God for **FAMILY**:

- How can you show your gratitude to God and to your relatives for the family He gave you?

- What are some memories you have that you can be thankful for and pass down to generations to come?

- What specific things can you do to geneate a spirit of thankfulness to God within your entire family?

My Thankful Life

_____

_____

_____

_____

_____

_____

_____

_____

_____

_____

_____

_____

_____

_____

_____

_____

_____

_____

_____

_____

_____

_____

_____

_____

_____

_____

_____

_____

_____

_____

My Thankful Thoughts

_____

_____

_____

_____

_____

_____

_____

_____

_____

_____

_____

_____

_____

_____

_____

_____

(place your church photo here)

CHURCH

"Just as each of us has one body with
many members, and these members do not
all have the same function, so in Christ
we who are many form one body, and each
member belongs to all the others."
- Romans 12:4-5

For me, my church family was an extension of my immediate family. My church had a real sense of community, and it was in this place and with these people that I learned to follow Christ.

The church is not perfect; it can't be because it's made up of imperfect people. It is, however, a place to receive strength, comfort and encouragement. Right now, my wife and I are involved in our church and our Sunday School class. I believe that in order for churches to grow, they must teach people how to build relationships. Relationships are what life is all about. We are created to love God and, in turn, love others. Recently, the men in my Sunday School class went out to eat and bowling. We had a good time and some new guys were able to get to know others. It is really through the time away from class that you get to know people. In the past, when my wife was sick, a few of the ladies came over to our house with some food for our family. They encouraged my wife so much during that time of sickness, bringing not only physical food but spiritual food, as well.

Nine years ago, I lived across the street from a neighbor whose wife died suddenly of lung cancer. He did not have a church family. With little to no support, it was difficult for him to deal with that loss. I watched as he, along with his family and friends, drank alcohol excessively in an attempt to wash away their pain. I knew those actions would only provide temporary relief instead of sustained comfort. Therefore, my wife and I invited him to our church. He rode with us the first time, but he soon began to come on his own. Shortly thereafter, he accepted Jesus Christ as his Savior and was baptized. He is now remarried, and he and his wife are both actively involved in our church.

Author's Thankful Thoughts

I am thankful for a place to worship God and
fellowship regularly. It makes such a difference
in my daily life knowing that other believers are
praying for me and are there to support me. I am not
only thankful for my church, but also for all the
Christians across the country and throughout the
world who are actively pursuing the way of Christ.
I remember when I met a gentleman from Sudan who
asked to take a picture of me so the churches in
Sudan could see for whom they were praying. See,
the church is literally one unified body, made up
of all types of people with a common purpose - to
bring glory to Jesus Christ by meeting the needs of
others. Church is not a building, but people, and
each member is vitally important. I am thankful for
the entire body of Christ as we pray for and support
one another.

Go Deeper: 1 Corinthians 12:12-31, Acts 2:42-47

Points to consider as we thank God for **CHURCH**:

- How is God using your church to reach out to others? Be thankful for these ministries.

- How has the family of God (the universal Church) been a blessing to you personally?

- In what ways can you show your thankfulness to God for His church (ex. giving of your time, talents, and/or money)?

My Thankful Life

_____

_____

_____

_____

_____

_____

_____

_____

_____

_____

_____

_____

_____

_____

_____

_____

_____

_____

_____

_____

_____

_____

_____

_____

_____

_____

_____

_____

_____

_____

_____

My Thankful Thoughts

_____

_____

_____

_____

_____

_____

_____

_____

_____

_____

_____

_____

_____

_____

_____

HEALTH

"Dear friend, I pray that you may
enjoy good health and that all may
go well with you . . ."
— 3 John 1:2

When I was 22 years old and just seven months out of college, I noticed some type of growth in the back of my mouth next to my salivary gland. It looked a little strange, so I scheduled a visit with a doctor in Virginia, where I was working at the time. This first doctor did not think it was anything to be concerned about: probably scar tissue built up from years of wearing braces. However, after I spoke to my mother about it, she scheduled another appointment for me with a doctor in Greensboro, NC. I saw him on Tuesday, and I was on the operating table that Friday. The report was malignant carcinoma – cancer. I was only 22! While it was hard to give thanks for the situation at the time, looking back, I am so thankful for that time because it helped me understand many important things in life:

1.) I must have a listening heart. Had I not followed my mother's guidance, I may not be here today.

2.) I drew closer to the Lord with long walks and journaling. I learned that God wants me to draw near to Him daily, and "He will draw near to me" (James 4:8).

3.) I have been able to talk to others about their health issues and relate to them in a way that I never would have been able to before.

Author's Thankful Thoughts

I am thankful for my health. I no longer take it for granted since it was almost taken from me at the young age of 22. Diseases like cancer strike fear in the hearts of so many. But we have been created to bring glory to God no matter how long He allows us to live on this earth. Each day is a gift from God. What we do with each day is simply our gift back to Him.

Go Deeper: 2 Kings 20:1-7, 2 Corinthians 1:8-11

Points to consider as we thank God for **HEALTH**:

- What health concerns has God brought you or a loved one through that you can thank Him for right now?

- How can you use the health God has given you to better serve Him?

- Think of ways that God might use even illness to teach you, and thank Him for being with you in sickness as well as health.

My Thankful Life

_____

_____

_____

_____

_____

_____

_____

_____

_____

_____

_____

_____

_____

_____

_____

My Thankful Thoughts

_____

_____

_____

_____

_____

_____

_____

_____

_____

_____

_____

_____

_____

_____

CLOTHES

"And why do you worry about clothes? See how the lilies of the field grow. They do not labor or spin. Yet I tell you that not even Solomon in all his splendor was dressed like one of these. If that is how God clothes the grass of the field, which is here today and tomorrow is thrown into the fire, will he not much more clothe you, O you of little faith."
— Matthew 6:28-30

Clothes are such a basic need. In America, we often forget that it is a struggle for many people across the world to clothe themselves. I remember, when I was a young boy, being so excited about my upcoming birthday. I really wanted a new football game for my birthday. But when you grow up in a family of six (four boys, along with my mom and dad), a practical gift is often more important. Well, my birthday came, and I got a pair of pants and a shirt. I was so upset that I did not get the game I wanted. I still remember the feeling of disappointment. However, today I am so thankful for those pants. I still have a photo in my office of my three brothers and me, and in that picture I am wearing those striped pants! I have to admit…I was looking pretty cool! I cherish that photo because it reminds me of how my parents sacrificed to put clothes on my back. I know they would have gotten me the game if they could have afforded to, but they knew it was not a necessity at that time. Money was tight, and they made the right decision to provide for my needs.

Author's Thankful Thoughts

I am thankful for the clothes God provides for me now and the clothes He provided for me as a child. I am also thankful that, through my parents' sacrifice, He taught me the value of having clothes.

I understand that even more now because I am a parent of two young children. The world is consumed with having the top fashions, and often people become discouraged when they cannot afford the most stylish clothes. But God says He will provide, not all of our wants, but all of our needs. And we can always thank Him for that.

Go Deeper: Matthew 6:25-34, 1 Timothy 6:6-8

Points to consider as we thank God for **CLOTHES**:

- If you have clothes on your back (or access to them) as you read this book, be thankful!

- Are you content with what God has provided for you or do you want more? Remember to thank Him for providing for your basic needs.

- How can you help provide clothing for others who may be in need?

My Thankful Life

_____

_____

_____

_____

_____

_____

_____

_____

_____

_____

_____

_____

_____

_____

_____

_____

SHELTER

"He who dwells in the shelter of the
Most High will rest in the shadow of
the Almighty."
— Psalm 91:1

In 1990, I went to speak at a basketball camp in Vermont. The campsite where the players and coaches stayed was in a very remote place. I remember asking the driver who picked me up at the airport where we were. You see, I did not know the gentleman and we had been on a dirt road for a long time. Was I in danger? No, there were just a lot of dirt roads in Vermont back in 1990.

He took me to the place I was staying: a large Victorian house with no hot water and a nightly raccoon and rat problem! Now I know why I was the only one staying in the house! Even though those things made my stay a bit uncomfortable, I am thankful for the week I stayed there. It was during that time with no TV, cold showers, and the possibility of some nighttime adventure, that I really began to use my time more wisely. You see, I did not want to stay in that house any more than I had to, so I would get up at sunrise and take long walks. During those walks I would pray, think, and reflect on God's blessings in my life, especially the young lady I was dating (and eventually married). I also had time to think about and prepare speeches I would be giving later in the day. I learned that I was often guilty of bringing distractions into my home and life when what I really needed was to spend time with God so I could grow deeper in my relationship with Him and my understanding of His shelter.

Author's Thankful Thoughts

I am thankful for the shelter I had that week. Even though it wasn't much to look at, that old house meant a lot to me because God used it to make me focus on more important issues in my life. God is our shelter, our rock, our strength and refuge.

Go Deeper: Psalm 46, Matthew 7:24-27

Points to consider as we thank God for **SHELTER**:

- If you have a roof over your head and a place to go when you need a refuge, thank God for physical shelter.

- Are you more dependent on your physical shelter or the spiritual shelter God provides?

- When did you last take time to truly rest in the shelter of the Lord? Thank Him for being that safe haven you can always run to.

My Thankful Life

_____

_____

_____

_____

_____

_____

_____

_____

_____

_____

_____

_____

_____

_____

_____

My Thankful Thoughts

_____

_____

_____

_____

_____

_____

_____

_____

_____

_____

_____

_____

_____

_____

_____

CHOICES

"Be strong and very courageous. Be careful to obey all the law my servant Moses gave you; do not turn from it to the right or to the left, that you may be successful wherever you go."
— Joshua 1:7

Friends are either a positive or a negative influence. I remember a time in my life when I had to make a difficult decision not to follow my friends. It can be a very lonely existence when your friends choose to go one way and you choose another. For example, when I was in college and my friends would ask me to go out on the town, I chose not to join them. Not only did I have my character to protect, but my dad was adamant about not paying my tuition if I ever got in trouble while in college. So while part of my decision was influenced by my morals, I also had the fear of my father and his potential consequences.

Those nights would be very lonely, but in my heart I knew I had made the right choice.

Later in life, I had a friend who was getting married. The night before his wedding, some guys chose to take him to a gentleman's club. Because of my lifestyle and the choices I had made in the past, they did not ask me to go, and for that I am very thankful. On the day of his wedding, my friend was sick and felt guilty the entire day because of the choice he had made.

Author's Thankful Thoughts

I am thankful for the friends I had in college, but I am also thankful for the times I chose to do what was right over following the crowd. Our character and reputation take a long time to build up, but can quickly be destroyed by a bad decision. God gives us the ability to choose what is best for our lives by reading His Word and by praying about every decision. Even where there is not a clear answer, He promises to guide us in our choices.

Go Deeper: Deuteronomy 30: 15-20, Joshua 24:14-18, 1 Kings 18:21

Points to consider as we thank God for **CHOICES**:

- Are you abusing the capability God has given you to make your own decisions by choosing things that do not honor Him? In our thankfulness, let us not take advantage of the privilege.

- Your choices do have an effect on people are they influencing others positively by reflecting Christ?

- Be thankful for the fact that God is always with you in whatever decisions you need to make.

My Thankful Life

_____

_____

_____

_____

_____

_____

_____

_____

_____

_____

_____

_____

_____

_____

_____

My Thankful Thoughts

_____

_____

_____

_____

_____

_____

_____

_____

_____

_____

_____

_____

_____

_____

_____

(place your photo of friends here)

FRIENDSHIP

"A man of many companions may come
to ruin, but there is a friend who
sticks closer than a brother."
— Proverbs 18:24

I've had the privilege of having wonderful friends throughout my life: friends who are fun, encouraging, and loyal. For example, I can remember going to the beach with two of my friends one spring. Initially, the weather was beautiful, but it quickly changed to cold and rainy in a matter of hours. Unfortunately for us, the heat had been turned off in the house we were staying in that week. But did we leave? No! We simply wore toboggans, long pants, and jackets while we played Uno and Monopoly for three days straight! We had a great time talking, laughing and enjoying each other's company. It was good conversation, fellowship, and competition among three very competitive friends. Some people may not consider that a good time since there was no alcohol, TV, or video games, but to me it was clean fun with no regrets or bad memories.

You know you have a good friend when the two of you go through the fire together and still have one another's backs. Sometimes you do not find out who your true friends are until some sort of crisis takes place in your life. I remember when I was coaching high school basketball with my good friend. Initially we were just coaching together, but we ended up being great friends. We had to make some difficult decisions that year regarding which kids would be on the varsity team. It was always hard for me to make cuts on an athletic team; nevertheless, it had to be done. The other coach and I made the cuts we thought were appropriate, but they were not very popular with some of the parents, as you can imagine. We took a lot of heat from different directions, but we stuck with our decision because it was what we felt was best for the team and the entire program. As friends, we had to stick together because others were trying to change our minds and get us to reconsider. In fact, if my friend had not been a true friend, he could have easily said it was all my idea, placed the blame on me, or tried to hurt my name and character. Instead, we made the choice to support one another.

```
Author's Thankful Thoughts

Looking back, I am so thankful for that experience.
We have been friends for 19 years. We went through
the fire and came out stronger than ever. I am
thankful for genuine friends like him. God created
us to develop relationships with others, and I can
give thanks for all the friends the Lord has given
me: friends with whom I can spend time, encourage,
and even compete. Of course, God is the best friend
I could ever have!

Go Deeper: John 15:12-15, Proverbs 27:6,17
```

Points to consider as we thank God for **FRIENDSHIP**:

- Have you recently thanked your friends for simply being your friends?

- What kind of friend are you to those who call you friend?

- Is your friendship with God closer than your friendship with others?

_____

_____

_____

_____

_____

_____

_____

_____

_____

_____

_____

_____

_____

_____

_____

_____

_____

_____

_____

_____

_____

_____

_____

_____

_____

_____

_____

_____

_____

_____

My Thankful Thoughts

_____

_____

_____

_____

_____

_____

_____

_____

_____

_____

_____

_____

_____

_____

_____

_____

TECHNOLOGY

"They said to each other, 'Come, let's make bricks and bake them thoroughly.' They used brick instead of stone, and tar for mortar. Then they said, 'Come, let us build ourselves a city, with a tower that reaches to the heavens, so that we may make a name for ourselves and not be scattered over the face of the whole earth.' But the LORD came down to see the city and the tower that the men were building. The LORD said, 'If as one people speaking the same language they have begun to do this, then nothing they plan to do will be impossible for them.'"

— Genesis 11:3-6

When I think about the computers we have today, along with all the other forms of technology, it is absolutely amazing how far we have come! I started my sports management company in the fall of 1994, and it was then that I bought my first computer. It was a used computer I found in a local newspaper classified ad. I thought, Wow, I am really in business now! Unfortunately, I soon discovered my computer (that I thought was so great) could not download or install AOL, and it didn't have very much memory space either. What was memory anyway? I thought only we (humans) had memory. Of course I had to buy a new computer then and, since 1994, many more as well. I now have a hand-held phone that receives all of my email. As technology has evolved, it has helped me to be more productive. I am very thankful. I am also thankful for how technology has helped spread the good news of Jesus Christ throughout the world. For example, ministries and groups can teach and equip missionaries anywhere through online teaching guides, Bible classes can be taken online from all around the world, and Biblical research is unlimited. In my opinion, technology has broken down more walls than any single thing in this century!

```
┌ ─ ─ ─ ─ ─ ─ ─ ─ ─ ─ ─ ─ ─ ─ ─ ─ ─ ─ ─ ─ ─ ─ ─ ─ ─ ─ ┐
│                                                     │
│           Author's Thankful Thoughts               │
│                                                     │
│                                                     │
│   I am so thankful for the technological advances we│
│   have made and pray that we use what we know to help│
│   others. I believe technology is a gift from God. But│
│   as the Bible says, „To whom much is given, much is │
│   required" (Luke 12:48). It is important for us to  │
│   realize that we have a responsibility to use the   │
│   gifts we have for the good of others, especially   │
│   to spread the message of Christ.                   │
│                                                     │
│   Go Deeper: James 1:17                             │
│                                                     │
└ ─ ─ ─ ─ ─ ─ ─ ─ ─ ─ ─ ─ ─ ─ ─ ─ ─ ─ ─ ─ ─ ─ ─ ─ ─ ─ ┘
```

Points to consider as we thank God for **TECHNOLOGY**:

- Has technology been a blessing (used for the advancement of the cause of Christ) or a curse (distracting you from Christ) in your life?

- How can you use the technological progress in our society to reach out to others?

- Consider the opportunities we have because of technology that others in different parts of the world may not have. Do not take that for granted.

_____

_____

_____

_____

_____

_____

_____

_____

_____

_____

_____

_____

_____

_____

_____

_____

My Thankful Thoughts

_____

_____

_____

_____

_____

_____

_____

_____

_____

_____

_____

_____

_____

_____

_____

LITERACY

"But he said to me, 'My grace is
sufficient for you, for my power is made
perfect in weakness.' Therefore I will
boast all the more gladly about my
weaknesses, so that Christ's power may
rest on me. That is why, for Christ's
sake, I delight in weaknesses, in
insults, in hardships, in persecutions,
in difficulties. For when I am weak,
then I am strong."
- 2 Corinthians 12:9-10

When I was about six years old, I began to go to speech class at a local college. My reading skills were not quite up to par because my speech needed some work. I remember not wanting to read out loud because I had trouble pronouncing words the right way. However, with intervention from others and hard work on my part, I was able to overcome the difficulties I had. Because of the help I obtained, today I am not only an avid reader, but a speaker as well. In fact, as I write this book, I am on my way to do two television interviews and will also speak at a university awards event. God has brought me a long way.

```
Author's Thankful Thoughts

I am thankful for the speech teacher who gave of her
time to help me learn to read and speak properly. I
am also thankful for my parents noticing that I
needed help and for reading all those stories to me
over the years in order to sharpen my skills. Now,
as I use the skills God has developed in me, I only
hope to bring Him glory.

Go Deeper: Deuteronomy 17:18-19, 1 Timothy 4:13
```

Points to consider as we thank God for **LITERACY**:

- Literacy is a basic part of life that we often take for granted.

- Since you are reading and understanding this book, you clearly have some sense of literacy. Think of those who have helped you acquire these skills (teachers, family, friends, coaches/ therapists, etc). Are you thankful to for them? Have you told them?

- How are you using your ability to read and write to glorify the Lord and advance His Kingdom?

_____

_____

_____

_____

_____

_____

_____

_____

_____

_____

_____

_____

_____

_____

_____

_____

_____

_____

_____

_____

_____

_____

_____

_____

_____

_____

_____

_____

My Thankful Thoughts

_____

_____

_____

_____

_____

_____

_____

_____

_____

_____

_____

_____

_____

_____

HELP

"Learn to do right! Seek justice,
encourage the oppressed. Defend the
cause of the fatherless, plead the
case of the widow."
— Isaiah 1:17

The word "help" has little meaning today because it is so overused. We often say to other people, "Call me if I can help you." Most of the time we really don't mean what we say. At a very young age I was taught the true meaning of help. My dad would volunteer his boys to help widowed ladies at our church or in our neighborhood. He taught us that if you say you are going to help someone, make it a priority, not just a casual use of the word. Through this, I learned that I need to put action behind my good intentions because as the Bible says, "faith without works is dead."

Recently, a friend of mine was moving into a new neighborhood. He asked me to help him move all of his furniture, so we started at 8:00 am one Saturday morning. I wasn't sure how much help he had enlisted when I first agreed, but come to find out, there were only three of us! We had a big job ahead of us, not because there was a lot to move, but because later that day he was throwing a surprise 40th birthday party for his wife in their new home! Wow!

Moving day is a pretty messy day at a new house, but we really wanted to come through for him. My other friend and I did not want him to end up in the dog house with his wife! So we moved everything, mowed the grass, edged the yard, washed the floors, put the beds together, vacuumed the entire house and then came back later for the party! I am so thankful I was able to help. My buddy's wife was so happy and proud of her new home...and she had a wonderful party, too!

Author's Thankful Thoughts

I have found that when you go out and help others, you are the one who actually receives the blessing. Our world is full of needy people. We are commissioned by God to be full time ministers for Him, helping meet the needs of others whenever we have the opportunity. We are His hands and feet on this earth. God tells us to love sacrificially, as Christ loves us, and that love is shown by what we do.

Go Deeper: Matthew 25:40, Acts 20:34-35, Hebrews 6:10

Points to consider as we thank God for **HELP**:

- Think of how much our Lord has helped and continues to help us. Do you help others with the same spirit as Christ does?

- Are you putting yourself in positions where God can use you to help others?

- What specific things has God helped you with lately, and did you thank Him?

My Thankful Life

_____

_____

_____

_____

_____

_____

_____

_____

_____

_____

_____

_____

_____

_____

_____

_____

My Thankful Thoughts

_____

_____

_____

_____

_____

_____

_____

_____

_____

_____

_____

_____

_____

_____

_____

(place your neighbors photo here)

NEIGHBORS

"Love the Lord your God with all your
heart and with all your soul and with
all your mind and with all your strength.
The second is this: Love your neighbor as
yourself. There is no commandment
greater than these."
— Mark 12:30-31

My family and I live beside Lavone Howard. She is over 80 years young. She is so sweet and kind to our family. When I stop and think about the benefits of living beside someone like her, the list becomes endless. Lavone is still in good health. She mows, blows, and gardens her 2.5 acre lot all by herself. What an inspiration that is in itself! Having her as a neighbor has also allowed me to model for my children the way we are supposed to help widows. My dad taught me this valuable principle, and now I am able to teach it to my children, as well. My family and I visit Lavone and her dog, Cody, often. We help her out, and she knows she can call me anytime. For my kids, it's like having another grandmother next door. If Lavone is out in the yard, they will run over and give her a big hug. They love spending time with her. By the way, she makes great passion pie and cranberry bread!

Author's Thankful Thoughts

I believe that God puts us in a specific place for a reason. I am so thankful the Lord put us beside Lavone Howard. It has sincerely been a blessing to have such a sweet lady next door to our family. I truly feel that having her next door has helped my children grow spiritually. Of course, our neighbors spread beyond the houses that might be next door to us. They are all around us—those who share this journey of life with us. But regardless of who we call our neighbors, God has placed them in our lives for a purpose, and we should be thankful for the relationships we can build with them.

Go Deeper: Leviticus 19:16–18, Proverbs 3:28–29, Luke 10:25–37

Points to consider as we thank God for **NEIGHBORS**:

- Ask God why he has placed you where you are. How can you minister to those around you?

- Is there anyone you should thank for being a good neighbor?

- Do you truly love your neighbors as yourself?

My Thankful Life

_____

_____

_____

_____

_____

_____

_____

_____

_____

_____

_____

_____

_____

_____

My Thankful Thoughts

_____

_____

_____

_____

_____

_____

_____

_____

_____

_____

_____

_____

_____

_____

_____

(place your photo of your home here)

HOME

"From one man he made every nation of men, that they should inhabit the whole earth; and he determined the times set for them and the exact places where they should live."

— Acts 17:26

In my lifetime, I have only lived in two states, Virginia and North Carolina. I've spent seven years total in Virginia, four years of college and three years during my first job. The rest of my life has been spent in North Carolina. My current job requires me to travel all over the country, but when I get back to North Carolina, I know I am home.

North Carolina is such a beautiful state. I call it the California of the east. We have mountains, ski slopes, lakes and fishing, beautiful beaches, and great weather during all four seasons. Most of us do not think about being thankful for the state in which we live until we have traveled to different states or other countries. I'm not being critical of other states because I love our entire country and its diversity. I guess I'm just partial towards my home state. I think it's okay to be that way no matter where you live. The state of North Carolina has so many wonderful places to visit. I have fond memories of going to places like Tweetsie Railroad, Grandfather Mountain, and Johnny Mercer Pier in Wrightsville Beach. I remember one trip in particular. My dad had taken his three oldest boys fishing at the pier in Wrightsville Beach. We fished most of the night. Listening to the ocean at night and looking out only to see darkness can put even the best fisherman to sleep. We began to drive back to my grandmother's house, but after a long night of fishing even my dad got a little sleepy. He stopped at the perfect location for coffee and doughnuts—Krispy Kreme! For my brothers and me, it was a big deal to fish all night and then stop at Krispy Kreme on the way back. We thought we were big boys for sure! When we finally got back to my grandmother's house in LeLand, North Carolina, my dad made an executive decision to make us sleep in the car for the rest of the night. He did not want us to wake up my mother, grandmother, and youngest brother (who was too young to go on the trip). Well, I thought sleeping in the car was a really cool idea! However, after about an hour of trying to get comfortable in between four people, breathing in the hot, humid air, and dealing with the mosquitoes, I decided sleeping in the car really wasn't that cool after all. When morning came, I was pretty happy!

```
┌─────────────────────────────────────────────────────┐
│                                                     │
│            Author's Thankful Thoughts               │
│                                                     │
│  I am very thankful I have had an opportunity to live │
│  in NC and make my home here. I am thankful for the  │
│  places I've been able to visit throughout my state  │
│  and the wonderful memories I'll always treasure. I  │
│  am thankful now that my kids can also participate in │
│  a lot of the great activities in the state of North │
│  Carolina. The feeling of having a place to belong,  │
│  a place that just feels right, is irreplaceable.    │
│  And God's children can look forward to our eternal  │
│  dwelling place. There truly is no place like home.  │
│                                                     │
│  Go Deeper: Psalm 84, Proverbs 27:8, Isaiah 32:18    │
│                                                     │
└─────────────────────────────────────────────────────┘
```

Points to consider as we thank God for **HOME**:

- What aspects of your home (town/city, state, etc.) do you love most?

- Do you treasure memories you've made in your home with a heart of gratitude toward God?

- When was the last time you thanked God for the home he has prepared for you in heaven?

My Thankful Life

_____

_____

_____

_____

_____

_____

_____

_____

_____

_____

_____

_____

_____

_____

_____

My Thankful Thoughts

_____

_____

_____

_____

_____

_____

_____

_____

_____

_____

_____

_____

_____

_____

(place your mentors photo here)

MENTORS

"For you know that we dealt with each
of you as a father deals with his
own children, encouraging, comforting
and urging you to live lives worthy
of God, who calls you into his
kingdom and glory."
— 1 Thessalonians 2:11-12

Webster defines a mentor as a wise, loyal advisor; a teacher or coach. Mentors can be very hard to find. I have never really had someone spend time to mentor me personally, but I have had people in my life who have demonstrated ways to perform certain tasks, how to handle various situations, and how to make a difference for others in this world. Because of my strong relationship with my dad, he could be considered my mentor. He spent many hours talking to me about business and ideas. Just yesterday I gave him a packet of information on a potential business opportunity to review for me. In my opinion, mentoring is a simple concept: give a little time to help others along on their journey. Hopefully, as a Christian, others will see who your true mentor is in life and who you are trying to imitate Jesus Christ. Ephesians 5:1 tells us to "be imitators of God" since we are His dearly loved children. If we strive to be more like Him, we will indeed have someone who will not fail us or let us down. The Bible says that "He will never leave us or forsake us" (Hebrews 13:5b). Right now, not only do I have an opportunity to be a father to my children, but also a mentor. I want them to know their true mentor is Jesus Christ and they should seek to imitate Him in all ways because "whoever claims to know Him, must walk as He did" (1 John 2:6).

```
Author's Thankful Thoughts

I am thankful that I can mentor my children. What
an honor! It is a deep commitment and challenge to
mentor and teach your children, but it is such a
worthy task. I am also thankful for my father who
mentored me over the years and continues to guide
and influence me today.

Go Deeper: Deuteronomy 3:28, 2 Kings 2:1-15,
Psalm 25:4-5,9, Proverbs 1:1-9
```

Points to consider as we thank God for **MENTORS**:

- Think of one or more people who have guided you at some point in life. Make a commitment to thank them for their direction and support.

- How can you be a mentor to someone else right now? Are you going and making disciples as the Bible commands us (Matthew 28:16-20)?

- Do you consider Christ to be a mentor in your life? If so, are you following his leadership?

My Thankful Life

My Thankful Thoughts

_____

_____

_____

_____

_____

_____

_____

_____

_____

_____

_____

_____

_____

_____

_____

_____

SANITATION

"A man who is clean shall gather up
the ashes of the heifer and put them
in a ceremonially clean place
outside the camp."
— Numbers 19:9

Wow! This is something we probably don't think about a lot. We just expect it in America. Our trash is collected and taken away, our restrooms function properly, and we have clean drinking water and a safe sewage system. As a kid, my brother always used to say he was going to be a garbage man. He thought it was so cool that they got to ride on the back of the truck and hold on while standing up. (I think he liked it in part because he knew it was something our parents would never let us do on their cars.) Today, however, most trucks are automated and pick up the trash cans from your home with what I like to call "the big claw." When we first moved into our home, there was so much work that needed to be done and we ended up creating a lot of garbage those first days. There was so much trash that I just knew those sanitation workers really hated coming to our house. I remember one day I was at home and had a really big load tons of trash! I looked out the window and saw the garbage men looking at all the stuff in disbelief. I knew what they were thinking, Are we really going to take all of this? So I hurried outside and began helping them load the truck with all my trash. That seemed to spur them on, and they hauled off all my trash that day. In gratitude, I gave them a snack and some Gatorade. I wanted them to know that their work was appreciated. Since then, they have always taken all my trash away, regardless of how much there is.

Author's Thankful Thoughts

I am so thankful for all the sanitation we have in America. My desire is to help keep our nation clean. I believe God wants us all to make the effort to take care of the valuable resources He has given us. On a more personal note, I am also thankful for those guys that come to my house every week to pick up my garbage.

Go Deeper: Leviticus 6:28, Leviticus 11, Numbers 19

Points to consider as we thank God for **SANITATION**:

- Have you been taking the sanitation you enjoy for granted?

- What specific things can you do to show your gratitude for those who look after sanitation issues for you?

- How can you do your part to take care of the resources God has blessed you with?

My Thankful Life

_____

_____

_____

_____

_____

_____

_____

_____

_____

_____

_____

_____

_____

_____

My Thankful Thoughts

_____

_____

_____

_____

_____

_____

_____

_____

_____

_____

_____

_____

_____

_____

_____

HOLY SPIRIT

"But the Counselor, the Holy Spirit, whom
the Father will send in my name, will
teach you all things and will remind you
of everything I have said to you."
— John 14:26

How do you write about the Holy Spirit? I mean, He is such a force in my life. It literally is Christ living in me (Galatians 2:20). It is also the convicting power that either keeps me from entering into sin or compels my heart toward repentance (turning away from a committed sin). I am so thankful I have the Holy Spirit dwelling within me.

Another function of the Holy Spirit is to lead and direct me in sharing my faith with other people. Just yesterday I was on a flight from North Carolina to California to do a television interview. I have always had a deal with the Lord: if He gives me an opportunity to go somewhere on business, I will use that flight to speak His name to those around me if given the chance. I feel that if the Lord blesses me in my business, then I need to use that flight as an opportunity to share with someone "the reason for the hope I have" (1 Peter 3:15) or to encourage another brother or sister in Christ. I have to say, what Christ has done on my last three flights has been absolutely amazing.

Flight #1 – A young lady sitting beside me was visibly upset. After a few minutes, I asked her how she was doing, even though I knew it wasn't good. It is amazing how many hurting people there are in our world today. She went on to share her pain with me. She was originally from India but had been working in the United States for the past three years. Using my Bible, I showed this young lady some encouraging verses about how much Jesus loves her. I had a couple of music CDs in my bag that someone had given me prior to my flight. They had uplifting, Christian songs on them, so I gave them to her. At first I thought that would be enough, but I felt the Holy Spirit urging me to give her my Bible, as well. She was unfamiliar with the Bible, so I am thankful the Holy Spirit impressed it upon my heart. I gave her my Bible, and she was so grateful. Only God knows where she went from there. I'm just thankful I could pass along God's Word to her during a difficult time in her life. I know I was obedient to what God wanted me to do.

Fight #2 – I sat down and the guy next to me was immediately very chatty. That made it easy to have conversation, so we talked the entire flight. We talked about our professions. I was able to share about faith and sports, while he was able to share about his line of work, electricity and electronics. As our conversation progressed, he told me that his wife was in bad health, so traveling was very hard on him because he didn't like leaving her. As we taxied to our gate, I told him that I believed the Lord was looking out for him and would meet their needs. His reply was, "I don't think He knows my name." Wow! The Holy Spirit gave me a tremendous opportunity to talk to him about Jesus, but since we were getting off the plane (and both in a hurry to catch our connecting flights), we traded business cards and promised to talk soon. When I got back into the office that week, I sent him a gift and a letter telling him that Jesus could know his name. He sent me a letter back saying he would read the material I sent and then pass it on to another. I am so thankful the Holy Spirit introduced me to this man and gave me the opportunity to share the Gospel with him. I don't know what happened to that gentleman or his wife, but I trust the results of the conversation I had with him to God. (1 Corinthians 3:6-8)

Flight #3 – As previously mentioned, I gave away my travel Bible. Before I left home for my next flight, I looked for a Bible to take with me and found a small New Testament with Psalms and Proverbs. I had no idea what to expect on my flight that day, but I honestly believe the Holy Spirit was reminding me to take a Bible. The flight from North Carolina to Los Angeles was over five hours! As I got my seat assignment, I felt the Holy Spirit say to me, "This is your seat." But I thought that since it was a long flight, it would be nice to have some extra room. So I approached the ticket counter at the gate to see if they had the emergency aisle available. "No," she said. Again, the Holy Spirit said to me in a still, small voice, "I gave you a seat." As I sat down on the plane, I discovered I was in the middle seat, which is where I had to sit for the next 5+ hours. Talk about cramped! This was not my seat of choice, but as I was about to find out, it was the one that was assigned to me from above. The flight was almost full, and sitting beside me was a young man holding a red Bible. So I said to him, "You are reading a good book there." He responded, "Really? I don't know. I want to read it so I can argue it better." He went on to say that he had never gone to church as a kid and had never read anything from the Bible. I asked what prompted him to read it. "Well, it is the most popular book of all time." I told him it would impact his life. He kind of laughed at the thought. We had some good dialogue and I showed him some scriptures that are practical for everyday living. We also talked about different translations of the Bible (he was reading the King James Version). In our Sunday School class, we had recently completed a study about how to share your faith. The church gave everyone a small New Testament with stickers on the front and back about how to lead someone to Jesus Christ. Well, this happened to be the Bible I had taken with me on this particular trip. Again, the Holy Spirit prompted me to give it away. I was not sure how the gentleman would receive it because he had already made it clear that he disagreed with its contents. But I offered it to him anyway, and he accepted it. As we departed he said, "Thanks." I may never know the impact my words had on that young man, but it was a privilege to encourage and educate him about God's Word. We are all "God's fellow workers, created in Christ Jesus to do good works, which God prepared in advance for us to do" (Ephesians 2:10)

Author's Thankful Life

I am so thankful for the Holy Spirit and His power to influence and direct my life. I am thankful that it is not me, but Jesus who orchestrates His plan in my life through the Holy Spirit (Proverbs 16:9). I am thankful God's plan is best and He desires to prosper me and not to harm me, to give me hope and a future (Jeremiah 29:11). I don't know where I would be without the work of the Holy Spirit in my life. For all these things, I am deeply humbled and thankful.

Go Deeper: Romans 8:26-27, Ephesians 1:13-14, 2 Peter 1:20-21, 1 John 4:13

Points to consider as we thank God for the
HOLY SPIRIT:

- How sensitive are you to the prompting of the Holy Spirit?

- Think of a time when you know you sensed the leading of the Holy Spirit.

- Make a commitment to thank God daily for the gift of His Spirit.

My Thankful Thoughts

_____

_____

_____

_____

_____

_____

_____

_____

_____

_____

_____

_____

_____

_____

_____

TALENTS AND GIFTS

"There are different kinds of gifts,
but the same Spirit. There are
different kinds of service, but the
same Lord. There are different kinds
of working, but the same God works all
of them in all men."
— 1 Corinthians 12:4-6

So many times we, as humans, put ourselves in a box. Someone hires us to do a job, they give us a job description, and that is what we do. As an employer, I think job descriptions have their place, but I am not particularly a big fan of them. I have never written a job description for my employees. Instead, they all are challenged with this mission: to accomplish goals and objectives, to have a vision about their area of responsibility, and to be flexible. The Bible is very specific about the spiritual gifts God gives to each of us. I have been told by others that my gifts are encouragement and servanthood. I truly enjoy serving and helping others. Maybe that is why being a sports agent, marketing person, and publisher of a magazine gives me great joy. It allows me to serve others and encourage them along the way. In the past, I coached high school basketball, and that also brought me immense satisfaction as I served the players in preparation, teaching, correction, and encouragement. I am so thankful for the gifts God has freely given me. But I do not believe the Lord puts us in a box and says, "That's all you're going to get. This is all I created you to do." I believe the Lord will open doors of opportunity and growth if we consistently make ourselves available to Him.

I also believe that God wants us to be proper stewards of our gifts, talents and passions. There is no question that He has given us specific skills and propensities towards certain areas of work Because He has blessed us with these abilities, we should develop them to their fullest potential. We are to use them to help and bless others. As Scripture teaches us, "to whom much is given, much is required" (Luke 12:48b). Let us all be fully aware that what we have been given is a gift from God, but what we do with these gifts is our gift back to Him. So whatever you like to do or whatever it is you're good at, "do it all for the glory of God"
(1 Corinthians 10:31) because that's all He desires from us.

```
+---------------------------------------------------------+
|              Author's Thankful Thoughts                 |
|                                                         |
|  God has formed and created each of us for a purpose    |
|  (Ephesians 2:10). I am thankful not only for what      |
|  the Lord has given me, but also what He will give       |
|  me as I continue to grow, serve others, and seek        |
|  to bring glory to His name.                            |
|                                                         |
|  Go Deeper: Matthew 25:15-30, Romans 12:3-8             |
|                                                         |
+---------------------------------------------------------+
```

Points to consider as we thank God for
TALENTS and **GIFTS**:

- Are you aware of the specific gifts God has given you?

- How are you using the talents and gifts that have been entrusted to you?

- What can you do to show thankfulness to God for how He has blessed you in this way?

_____

_____

_____

_____

_____

_____

_____

_____

_____

_____

_____

_____

_____

_____

_____

My Thankful Thoughts

_____

_____

_____

_____

_____

_____

_____

_____

_____

_____

_____

_____

_____

_____

_____

(place a photo of your loved one(s) here)

131 Living the Thankful Life

LOVE

"Love never fails."
- 1 Corinthians 13:8a

My wife and I will have been married 20 years as of June 1, 2011. I can't believe how fast time flies! I can still remember the first time I met her. We were at a mutual friend's wedding and Jacqui was one of the bridesmaids. Even though we attended the same college, we had never met one another. As it turns out, she and one of her friends had even been over to my apartment once, but that particular night I was out on another date. On the day of this wedding, Jacqui's plane was eight hours late, and no one was available to pick her up at the airport. So my roommate (who knew Jacqui) and I went to the airport to get her. We picked her up, and she slipped into the cab of the white pick-up truck. Judging by her actions, it was probably her first time in a pick-up truck. You see, Jacqui had grown up in New Jersey, about 45 minutes outside of Manhattan, NY. She was more used to cabs, subways, and cars. While traveling back to the church, Jacqui talked to my roommate but never really spoke to me. When I introduced myself, she said, "Oh," and continued to talk to my roommate. We didn't speak another word to each other for the rest of the weekend. However, God's plan was for us to meet again soon.

I was coaching high school basketball in Charlotte, NC and our state tournament was in Greensboro, NC. Since my parents were still living in Greensboro, I decided to spend the night with them after our game on Saturday. I got up as always on Sunday morning and attended church with my parents. The church was really full that morning, and there were very few seats available. I always sat with my parents, especially when I was growing up. Some things never change because there I was, 26 years old, and I was still looking to sit with my parents. But on this particular day, there was no seat near them. So for the first time in my life, I began looking for a seat elsewhere, and guess who I saw? That's right, Jacqui and her roommate! She had just moved to Greensboro and taken a job. Of course she did not remember me, but I certainly remembered her. She thought my name was James. (I guess I made a great first impression!) I told Jacqui and her roommate to call me if they needed anything since they were new to the area, and then we traded phone numbers. It was strange how Jacqui and her roommate ended up at church that morning. They were looking in the yellow pages for a church to attend and found one not too far from their apartment, so they decided to go there. I thank God for directing us both to that particular church on that particular day.

On the way out of the church that morning, my mother met both of the girls. Later in the day, before I left my parents' house, my mother came up to my room, sat on the bed and said, "You remember that girl, Jacqui?" After I said yes, my mother said, "Did you get her number?" I thought, I am 26 years old, almost 27, and she is asking me if I got that girl's number! But of course I said yes, and my mother replied, "Will you promise to call her? I feel something special about her." I complied. Since then, Jacqui has been, and continues to be, the love of my life. I guess God (and moms) do know best!

```
Author's Thankful Life

I am thankful for the loving relationship I have
with my beautiful wife. I am so grateful that God
allowed us to cross paths and ultimately brought us
together as a couple. I am also thankful for the
love my mother showed me by taking the time to share
her heart and the feelings she had toward Jacqui.
Love is the most powerful and driving emotion God
has given us. Because He has loved us, we are able
to love others completely, just as He created us
to do.

Go Deeper: John 15:9-17, 1 Corinthians 13,
1 John 4:7-21
```

Points to consider as we thank God for **LOVE**:

- Consider what life would be like with the absence of love.

- How are you showing love toward others?

- Thank God for the unconditional love He always offers.

My Thankful Thoughts

_____

_____

_____

_____

_____

_____

_____

_____

_____

_____

_____

_____

_____

_____

_____

IDEAS

"From the fruit of his lips a man is
filled with good things as surely as the
work of his hands rewards him."
– Proverbs 12:14

We have so many opportunities in America. Because of our democratic society, we are free to be creative thinkers. Creativity is such a vibrant dynamic to our American culture. We can come up with an idea, and a short time later, have a thriving business. I like to dream. Those who know me best would attest to my brain never ceasing to imagine, dream, explore, and create. Thus, I have had many ideas throughout my lifetime. I think I drive my wife crazy with all my different ideas. Some are implemented; others are not. Some are good ideas; others are better. However, I believe the most important thing is that we act on our ideas. The work is in the action! I am constantly working on multiple projects at the same time. But I've had my share of ideas that I failed to follow through with, and I now regret that.

For example, many years ago I was installing a new mailbox in my yard and it occurred to me that someone needed to invent a plastic, self-contained mailbox—one that would be simple to purchase and easy to install. A few years later, that plastic mailbox showed up in Lowe's and Home Depot stores, but it was not my invention. Someone else had taken action. I also once had an idea for a service to show home owners how to prepare their house for resale called "Design to Sell." Well, it is now a TV show on HGTV, but it is not my show. This book you are reading right now was an idea given to me by God. I awoke one night around 2 am with the idea to write an interactive book about thankfulness. This book is a direct result of an idea that came to me only a few months ago and was acted upon. I am thankful for sleepless nights when an idea comes to me and I begin to think, pray, and consider acting on it. I appreciate that God has been gracious enough to give us the ability to think for ourselves and come up with our own ideas.

```
┌──────────────────────────────────────────────┐
│           Author's Thankful Thoughts          │
│                                               │
│  I am thankful for creativity and that God is the most │
│  creative person ever (Job 38-41 and Psalm 19). Thank │
│  you Lord for the idea of this book and the energy you │
│  have given me to make it a reality to people across │
│  the world as we celebrate thankfulness.      │
│                                               │
│  Go Deeper: Proverbs 16:1-3, James 1:17       │
└──────────────────────────────────────────────┘
```

Points to consider as we thank God for **IDEAS**:

- God has given us our own individual minds for a purpose.

- How often do we take for granted the ability to think and create for ourselves?

- What are ways that you have used your ideas and creativity to honor God?

My Thankful Life

My Thankful Thoughts

SILENCE

"At daybreak Jesus went out
to a solitary place."
— Luke 4:42

Have you ever wondered where all the silence has gone? At my house I have two children, and my wife says silence is rare. We have so much noise these days! We have radios, cell phones, TVs, computers, iPods, DVD players, etc. We seem to overwhelm ourselves with noise. Even if we do get a rare, quiet moment, we are sometimes so uncomfortable with it that we find a way to make noise. Yet it is in the quiet times that Jesus often speaks to us. In fact, He clearly tells us in His Word to "be still and know that I am God" (Psalm 46:10). Elijah discovered this truth when God's presence surrounded and overwhelmed him in the silence (1 Kings 19:11-13).

There have been many times when I have awoken in the middle of the night to spend some time praying or reading. I have also tried to turn my car into a place of silence. When I am alone in my car, I seldom have my radio on for long periods of time. I'm not against the radio or music; I just like to use that time to listen, think, and pray so I can hear what the Holy Spirit is prompting me to do in my life. The time I have in my car over the many miles and long trips has truly been a blessing to me. I love the noise of my family, but it is of utmost importance for me to have quiet time to listen to my Father, too. For it's in these times that I am strengthened spiritually and able to discern the heart of God more clearly.

Author's Thankful Thoughts

I am so thankful for silence—a time to reflect, learn from God, hear His voice, and understand He wants me to do with my life on a daily basis. In the stillness, I can do this without any distractions. I am also thankful that God speaks to me when I put myself in a proper position to listen to Him.

Go Deeper: Job 6:24, Psalm 4:3-4, Psalm 131, Lamentations 3:25-26, Habakkuk 2:20

Points to consider as we thank God for **SILENCE**:

- Has the busyness and noise of your life interfered with you hearing from God?

- Do you have a place and time of silence where you are truly ready to listen to that sometimes still, small voice?

- Imagine that the God of the universe desires to meet you in a quiet place where He knows He has your undivided attention. Be thankful that He wants that kind of intimate relationship with you.

_____

_____

_____

_____

_____

_____

_____

_____

_____

_____

_____

_____

_____

_____

_____

_____

_____

_____

_____

_____

_____

_____

_____

_____

_____

_____

_____

_____

_____

_____

My Thankful Thoughts

FELLOWSHIP

"If we walk in the light, as He is in
the light, we have fellowship with one
another, and the blood of Jesus, His
Son, purifies us from all sin."
— 1 John 1:7

God has given us a wonderful opportunity to fellowship with those around us. It's important for us to take time out from the daily routines of life to spend time with loved ones. Vacations have been a prime time for me to do this in my life. I remember as a kid going to a place in Atlantic Beach, North Carolina. My family rented an entire house on the sound of the beach, off the Intercoastal Waterway. We had our whole family there, all six of us. I thought the house was so cool because it had a pier in the backyard where we could go fishing! One night my dad took us gigging for flounder. Another night my grandmother drove over and taught us all how to crab. My mother would cook either seafood from the market or whatever we had caught that day. We also went on mini sailfish boat rides around the sound. Atlantic Beach was a great place to go as a family. It was so great to just be together, and we made so many memories there. For example, I remember one specific time when I hooked a huge flounder. I mean huge! My entire family was yelling and screaming in excitement. As I pulled the flounder up, he was jumping around everywhere!. Somehow he managed to flail himself off my hook and fell back into the water. What a bummer! I wonder if anyone ever caught him. Despite that feeling of disappointment, I remember my vacations at Atlantic Beach fondly, and the recollections of those times bring a smile to my face even to this day.

Author's Thankful Thoughts

Looking back, I am so thankful for those days and the memories that were made on vacation with my family. The fellowship we shared, and still share, is priceless. Whether with friends of family, it is good (and even necessary sometimes) to get away from everyday life to join together with others for times of fun, relaxation, and camaraderie. Now that I am married and have children, I am thankful that we have family vacations and are making memories that will last forever, as well.

Go Deeper: Ecclesiastes 4:7-12, Acts 2:42-47, 1 John 1:3-7

Points to consider as we thank God for **FELLOWSHIP**:

- Are you truly thankful for the opportunities God gives us to connect with others?

- How do you use your times of fellowship to glorify God and grow closer to Him?

- Think of precious memories you may have of vacations or other times of fellowship with family and friends.

My Thankful Life

My Thankful Thoughts

_____

_____

_____

_____

_____

_____

_____

_____

_____

_____

_____

_____

_____

_____

_____

My Thankful Thoughts

EDUCATION

"Let the wise listen and add
to their learning . . ."
- Proverbs 1:5a

I have my masters degree in Sports Management, and that is the highest degree I think I will achieve. I love to learn, but I believe I am finished with formal education. To me, education is far more than attending high school, college, graduate school, etc. It is a way of life. For example, I am currently the publisher of Sports Spectrum Magazine, a Christian sports magazine. I had no formal training in journalism, English (just ask my employees), or anything related to publishing a magazine. I had to study, learn, and network quickly in order to gain some knowledge about the business. I believe the key is to be a lifelong learner. Just because you don't know anything about a certain subject doesn't mean you can't learn it. The magazine is one of many endeavors in my life that has required me to learn. I personally love challenging myself to learn new things—it's exciting.

There's another clear example of how informal education has played a key role in my life. I am an NFL contract advisor (also known as an agent for NFL players). When I started this company, US Sports Management Inc., I knew nothing about the NFL or its guidelines on agents, etc. However, after a lot of studying, I soon passed the NFLPA test and was certified as an NFL agent. Since that time, we have negotiated NFL contracts and endorsements for many players. I thoroughly enjoy being a part of this industry, but first I had to educate myself with all the state laws, guidelines, and a host of other rules and regulations. I am glad that God has given me the drive to be a life long learner. I am also thankful that I have not been afraid to try new things and teach myself when needed.

Author's Thankful Thoughts

I am so thankful that education in itself is not the key that it is what you do with what you know and learn, regardless of what kind of degree you may or may not have, that is of utmost importance.

Go Deeper: Proverbs 1:1-7, Proverbs 2, Proverbs 18:15, Proverbs 24:3-5

Points to consider as we thank God for **EDUCATION**:

- Reflect upon your education, both formal and informal.

- How are you using the knowledge you've gained to be more useful to God's Kingdom?

- When was the last time you simply thanked God for the capacity to learn and then to put that education into practice?

My Thankful Life

_____

_____

_____

_____

_____

_____

_____

_____

_____

_____

_____

_____

_____

_____

_____

_____

_____

_____

_____

_____

_____

_____

_____

_____

_____

_____

_____

_____

_____

_____

My Thankful Thoughts

WORK

"All hard work brings a profit, but mere
talk leads only to poverty."
- Proverbs 14:23

I remember when I got my first job. My boss brought me into his office, looked me in the eyes and said, "Walker, did you go to college?"

"Yes, sir."

"Did you get a degree?"

"Yes, sir."

(I was not sure where he was going with this.)

Then he said, "Get out of my office. Go do your job. If you hang yourself, I will come cut you down." What a great first day of work: no job description and no "to-do" list! I was dumbfounded for a moment, as you might expect. How do you direct athletics? Was there a book I could read to find out? Not exactly. So I began my career teaching seven classes a day, coaching three sports, and helping with fundraisers and other items, as well.

I remember that year well. I nearly exhausted myself. At one point in the year, we built a new soccer field and sowed the seed for it. We waited days and days for God to provide the rain, but none came. So I came up with an idea: call the fire department! They gave me permission to use the fire hoses from the warehouse in their station. I connected them, walked outside and began to water the field with a fire hose. If you've never done that, it is quite an experience! I'll give you a piece of advice: stay moving! Thank the Lord for the automated irrigation systems we have today!

As I reflect back on that first year of being an athletic director, I realize it was during this time that I learned so much about being a thinker, being creative, and working hard to get the job done without any excuses.

Author's Thankful Thoughts

I am thankful for my first job because it taught me patience, perseverance, and confidence that "I can do all things through Christ who gives me strength" (Philippians 4:13). As a carpenter, Jesus gave a perfect example of being a diligent worker. He was constantly working for the benefit of others. People will be able to learn a lot about you by the work that you do not just as an occupation but in life in general. It is not always where you are that is important, but rather what you do where you are. I am thankful for the opportunity to work as unto the Lord and not for men.

Go Deeper: Genesis 2:15, Proverbs 10:4-5, Colossians 3:23-24

Points to consider as we thank God for **WORK**:

- What do you consider to be your "work" on earth?

- Has there been a time when you've had to rely completely on the Lord to get you through the work you were doing? Did you thank Him?

- Are you working as unto the Lord and not for men?

My Thankful Thoughts

(place a photo of your favorite food here)

FOOD

"Then God said, 'Let the land produce
vegetation: seed-bearing plants and trees
on the land that bear fruit with seed
in it, according to their various kinds.'
And it was so. The land produced
vegetation: plants bearing seed according
to their kinds and trees bearing fruit
with seed in it according to their kinds.
And God saw that it was good."
— Genesis 1:11-12

Growing up in Greensboro, NC, my family always had a large garden. I can remember spending many hot summer days in the garden. Our Saturdays were not full of sleeping late and watching cartoons, but rising early in the morning and heading to the garden to work. Looking back, those were some great family times, and I learned many things. I certainly learned the value of food and to appreciate the work that goes into growing food.

My brothers and I often reminisce about the hot tiller smoke that would come by as you held up the bean plant to keep the rows cleaned out. We also talk about hoeing the weeds and picking the vegetables with our mom on those early mornings. I can remember everyone gathering in the kitchen later in the day because it had a window unit air conditioner. We would all sit down, turn on the black and white TV, and snap beans together. Sometimes it seemed like it took all day. Butter beans were the toughest because you had to snap so many open in order to fill up your bowl. My mother was there with us the whole time, snapping, talking and keeping all four of us boys in line.

I think it would be wonderful if every family could have a garden, whether small or large, to help teach their children the value of food. Personally, growing up with a garden and actually watching the process of how food goes from the ground and onto my plate was eye-opening. I learned values during that time about how to appreciate food more and waste food less.

Author's Thankful Thoughts

I am so thankful for those times in the garden. I am also thankful that I can now teach my kids the worth of food through my own small garden in our backyard. God promises to meet all of our needs, and this is one way He has chosen to meet my family's needs, both growing up and today. In America, we are so blessed to have access to so much food. We have grocery stores and restaurants on almost every corner. We have more than we even need in most cases. But all that we have comes from the Lord, and we must never forget that.

Go Deeper: Genesis 1:29-30, Psalm 104:14-15, John 4:30-38, 1 Timothy 6:8

Points to consider as we thank God for **FOOD**:

- Have you recently thanked God for providing this basic need for you?

- Do you ever take the availability of food for granted?

- What can you do to generate new appreciation for food in your family?

My Thankful Life

My Thankful Thoughts

(place your pets photo here)

ANIMALS

"You are to bring into the ark two
of all living creatures, male and
female, to keep them alive with you.
Two of every kind of bird, of every
kind of animal and of every kind of
creature that moves along the ground
will come to you to be kept alive."
- Genesis 6:19-20

While growing up, there were dogs, cats, rabbits, birds and fish in my family. Having some type of pet was a good thing for me as a kid. When I was 12, I wanted a dog very badly. Not just any dog, but a cocker spaniel. I am not sure why, but I had my mind made up that a cocker spaniel was exactly what I needed. My heart was set on it. My parents said they would allow us to get the dog only if I would be responsible for taking care of it.

Well, we began to look and soon found a beautiful blonde cocker spaniel. I actually got to pick him out myself. My parents required me to take full responsibility, so that meant I had to pay $100.00 for the dog with the money I had saved from mowing grass. (I also had to buy a lot of the dog food and pay for the vet bills.) I named my new dog Prince. He was AKC registered and was a great dog! As a kid, we had a wonderful time with Prince; he was quite funny. My mother made incredible homemade biscuits from scratch and Prince loved those biscuits! He would take one and eat it right away. Then, thinking of the future, he would immediately take another and go bury it in the backyard for later. What a smart dog! You could never get close to him if he had a biscuit because he would protest with a fierce growl. However, in all my efforts to take care of Prince, I forgot two of the most important elements: discipline and training. (This was before you could take your dog to PetSmart for obedience training.) I bought a book on how to train dogs, but Prince was a little high strung and I liked playing with him more than disciplining him. Needless to say, he didn't get much training. Sometimes he would get out of the fence by digging a hole. He would stay gone all night and return the next morning. We would mend the fence, but he would get out again and just run like a mad dog. The only way I could catch him was if I grabbed a piece of bologna and took off after him. I remember to this day waving the bologna, calling his name, and running as fast as I could. Oh, what the neighbors must have thought! Eventually Prince would give in to the bologna and we would go back home.

One night, though, while my dad was taking Prince for a walk, Prince got off the leash. He jumped the creek and was headed toward home when he crossed the road and got hit by a car. He died instantly. I remember my dad telling me that Prince was dead. I was upstairs combing my hair when he told me the awful news. I was so hurt. He was my dog. I paid the price for him, took care of him, and yet he was gone so fast. My dad buried Prince for me because he did not want me to see him in his damaged condition. Dad wanted me to remember Prince as he was when he was alive.

Looking back, I know that it must have been hard for my mom and dad to see me so upset. However, that experience taught me an extremely tough lesson on the value of discipline and training. Because Prince was never trained or disciplined, he had an early death. Still, I am so grateful for the time that I was able to spend with Prince as my pet.

Author's Thankful Life

I am thankful for my dog, Prince, because he taught me many lessons. The most significant one was the importance of discipline and training. Many times we flee, too, when Jesus is "chasing" us. We run away, not heeding His guidance and discipline, and therefore miss out on His blessings. Now that I have kids, I'm constantly focusing on training them in the way they should live. I've gotten them a pet so they'll learn to be responsible for it and gain the same values I did by having Prince. God created the animals for us, and He can use even something as simple as having a pet to teach us.

Go Deeper: Genesis 1:24-25, Genesis 9:8-17, Psalm 36:6, Psalm 50:10-12

Points to consider as we thank God for **ANIMALS**:

- Did you ever have an experience with a pet that taught you a valuable lesson?

- How do you treat the animals that God has created?

- What things about animals/pets can you thank God for?

_____

_____

_____

_____

_____

_____

_____

_____

_____

_____

_____

_____

_____

_____

_____

My Thankful Thoughts

_____

_____

_____

_____

_____

_____

_____

_____

_____

_____

_____

_____

_____

_____

_____

_____

(place your parent(s) photo here)

PARENTING

"Children, obey your parents in the Lord,
for this is right. "Honor your father
and mother"—which is the first
commandment with a promise— "that it
may go well with you and that you may
enjoy long life on the earth." Fathers,
do not exasperate your children;
instead, bring them up in the
training and instruction of the Lord."
– Ephesians 6:1-4

Now that I am a dad, I have come to find out that parenting is not an easy task. In fact, I would say it's the most challenging responsibility I have. However, it is the most gratifying opportunity. As a parent, you must make tough choices along the way. Some of them will impact your children positively; others will impact them negatively.

I remember a tough decision my parents made that impacted my life as a seven-year-old. Now, I do not recall all the details of this particular event, but the impact it had on me was huge, and I remember it like it was yesterday. My brothers and I were in Kmart with my mother one day. She was looking in one of the big jewelry bins. As she was shopping around, I put a pair of earrings in my pocket to give to the girl that lived next door to us. For some reason I thought this 13 or 14-year-old teenager would like a pair of earrings from her 7-year-old neighbor. We left the store without me mentioning anything, and when we got home, I put the earrings in a drawer in my room. My brothers and I then walked across the street to go to the park. While we were there, as any good mother would do, my mom went through our drawers (as she frequently did). I guess she was making sure we had not brought any insects, mud balls or other items into the house that did not belong. My mother found the earrings and immediately knew we had not paid for them. When we came home, my mother confronted my brothers and me. I could not lie (and knew I shouldn't even try). I told her I had taken the earrings. She scolded me, told me how disappointed she was in me, and then said those dreaded words: "Your father will deal with this when he comes home." I knew I was in big trouble! I did not want to go to jail. I am only seven, I thought!

When my dad got home and heard the story, he immediately called the store manager, explained what had happened, and told him that we were on our way to the store to make it right. This next part of the story I remember very well because it made such an impression on me. As we walked into the store, I was so afraid of what was going to happen. I had no idea what to expect. My dad and I walked to the jewelry area and met the manager. At that point I apologized, gave back the earrings, and the manager gave me a little speech. To be honest, I don't remember what he said. I was too scared. As my dad and I walked back to the car, all I could focus on was how relieved I was that it was all over. Sometimes being a parent isn't easy for the parents or the kids!

Author's Thankful Thoughts

I am thankful that my mom and dad, no matter how painful it was, made the decision to raise me properly. Their consistency in making the right decisions (even when they were tough) has had a profound impact on my life. As a parent, it is difficult to prepare your children to become respectable adults, but it is far worse not to be the parent your children need and deserve. Without the intervention of parents, the consequences are grave. Therefore, parents have the responsibility of molding their kids' hearts and shaping them to be like Christ. Of course, our Heavenly Father is the greatest example of a parent we could have. I couldn't be more thankful for Him!

Go Deeper: Proverbs 17:6, Colossians 3:20-21

Points to consider as we thank God for **PARENTING**:

- Reflect on the parents you have and the tough decisions they may have had to make while raising you. Are you thankful for them?

- If you are a parent now, are you raising your child to be like Christ? If you are not a parent, what kind of parent do you hope to be?

- How can you show your gratitude to God and to your parents for all they have done?

My Thankful Life

_____

_____

_____

_____

_____

_____

_____

_____

_____

_____

_____

_____

_____

_____

_____

_____

My Thankful Thoughts

_____

_____

_____

_____

_____

_____

_____

_____

_____

_____

_____

_____

_____

_____

DISCIPLINE

"The fear of the Lord is the beginning
of knowledge, but fools despise
wisdom and discipline."
— Proverbs 1:7

Have you ever been caught for doing something wrong? I think I got caught almost every time I was out of line, but now I'm thankful for that!

When I was 18 years old, I came home from college one weekend. My brother and I borrowed my dad's two-door Cutlass after cleaning it up earlier that day. You see, Dad had a deal with us boys: if you want to use the car, you have to clean it first. Well, my brother and I knew about this event taking place at the local high school we used to attend. As a matter of fact, there were also two young ladies we wanted to see that night who just happened to be going to this event. But my mom and dad told us we were not allowed to go over there that night. Well, we really wanted to see those girls! So we made our way over to the school, saw the girls, and offered to take them home. It was a very rainy night. We dropped one girl off at her house and began to take the other one home. My brother kept telling me to slow down, but of course I kept telling him to shut up. My girl was in the car and I didn't want to look bad in front of her! The two-lane country road was wet and very curvy. As we rounded a curve, I ran off the road a little. I jerked the car back on the road, which was a bad decision. The car went into a wild spin and ended up in a ditch. The car was wrecked and we were stuck. My brother was so panicked. He said, "Dad is going to really get us! I might as well run away into those woods right now." My girlfriend was fine, and thankfully no one was hurt. The problem was that we were in the middle of nowhere, and this was before everyone had cell phones. We had no way to get in touch with anyone. There were no lights, no stores, nothing just us and our car stuck in a ditch.

We saw a farm house up the road, so we made the long walk over and knocked on the door. A farmer answered, and he graciously came out with his tractor and pulled the car out of the ditch. We couldn't thank him enough. We started down the road again with the car covered in mud and a shaky tire. We took my girlfriend home and asked her to call our parents and tell them that we were running a little late. My brother and I decided we had to find a place to wash the car. There was no way we were going to take it home in that condition. (We had to clean it up and make it look at least a little better!) We were the only people at the do-it-yourself carwash at that time of night. We washed, rinsed, and put hot wax on the car in an attempt to get it extra clean (even though it was wrecked up front). When we got home my dad simply looked at us and said, "Put the keys and your license on my dresser." I replied, "But Dad." "No buts, just do it," he said sternly. I wanted to tell my parents about the wreck, but we did not get a chance. Dad did not even want to talk to us. So my brother and I went to sleep that night thinking our life as we knew it would be over once Dad saw his damaged car. We must have said we loved each other thirty times that night. That was one of the longest nights in my life. My mother came in early the next morning and calmly asked, "Why were you boys out past curfew?" As I began to explain, she looked out the window, saw the front of the car and immediately yelled for my dad. I knew we were goners then. Luckily, Dad was in the shower as my mother told him what happened with the car. My dad, who was usually pretty adamant about taking short showers to conserve water, took the longest shower of his life that morning. When he finally got out, he took my brother and me outside to review the damage. He told us we would have to pay for the repairs ourselves. The estimate was over $2,000! My brother and I were supposed to split it. Thankfully, my dad decided to have us pay the deductible on the insurance instead. (To this day, my brother thinks I owe him for his half since he was not driving and kept telling me to slow down.)

Author's Thankful Thoughts

That night my brother and I learned many valuable lessons. First, obey your parents. Secondly, don't ever try to be deceptive and hide things; be honest and upfront. Lastly, when you do make a mistake, take responsibility and fix it. We can laugh now about how we thought we would be grounded for life and never date or drive again. What we don't laugh about is how we were being protected. Just a few yards down from the ditch we landed in was Lake Townsend. We could have easily ended up in the lake instead of the ditch. God watched over us that night, and my parents' discipline kept us from doing something like that again. I am thankful for the farmer that pulled us out of the ditch that night so we did not have to call my dad! But overall, I am thankful for getting caught when I have done wrong because I have learned so much from those moments of correction and sometimes punishment. I hope I don't get away with anything that's wrong according to God's standards. His discipline is much harder to take than that of my parents when I was younger, but it is always used to instruct me. I am grateful for God's protection over us that night, keeping us free from injury and out of that big lake! He really is my shelter, refuge, fortress, deliverer and guide.

Go Deeper: Deuteronomy 8:1-5, Job 5:17-18, Proverbs 3:11-12, Proverbs 5:21-23, Hebrews 12:7-11

Points to consider as we thank God for **DISCIPLINE**:

- Did you ever experience discipline that hurt at the time but that you can be thankful for now?

- How do you respond to God's discipline, which is always meant for good?

- What can you do to remind yourself to be thankful for the discipline you receive?

My Thankful Life

My Thankful Thoughts

_____

_____

_____

_____

_____

_____

_____

_____

_____

_____

_____

_____

_____

_____

_____

GUIDANCE

"For this God is our God for ever
and ever; he will be our guide
even to the end."
— Psalm 48:14

When I decided to go to college, I had only been on two college campuses in my life. The college I chose to attend, Liberty University, was one I had never visited or even seen. I picked it the same way you would pick what to order at a restaurant; it sounded good, so I went for it. (I have to admit, I do not recommend choosing a college that way. I am fortunate that Liberty turned out to be such a great match for me.)

Upon entering school, I knew I wanted to play soccer in college. On the first day, I had to be on campus for a meeting in the hallway of the soccer dorm. My parents and I were running a little behind schedule that day, so I was late for the first meeting! The coach let me know I was late, too. He called me out by name, which was more than a little embarrassing and not the best way to meet my new teammates. After the meeting, my parents helped me move into my dorm room. Then they gave me a kiss and said their good byes. Once they left, I realized it was time to grow up fast and make some friends because I did not know where anything was on campus! The only places I was familiar with were the soccer field and my room. Fortunately, I met up with one of my teammates, and the two of us made our way to the dining hall together. He gave me some guidance and kind of showed me around campus, which made me feel a lot better and more comfortable with my surroundings. At least I knew where to get food!

Soccer practice was a lot different from what I was used to at the small high school I had attended. I will never forget the long runs we had to make through the mountains! My freshman year I was on the second team, also known as the JV team. I'm not sure we had an official name, but we practiced every day with the traveling team. One day, the JV team had a game against Longwood College, the only official game I ever played in during my college career. During that game, I hurt my ankle. I am not sure what the formal diagnosis was, but I spent a lot of time in the training room with my foot in a bucket of ice in the weeks that followed. When my sophomore year started, the coach made a decision to carry only enough players to travel. So before tryouts, we were told that many of last year's players may not make this year's team. Well, I was a part of the group that was cut. When I went to meet with the coach, he gave me some great advice and guidance when he asked, "Why not start officiating soccer? That will keep you close to the game." I had never really thought about it that much, but he told me who to call and gave me the number. The next thing I knew, I was a soccer referee. I soon began to referee basketball, as well. I really enjoyed it! I learned some valuable lessons about life through officiating, like how to deal with adverse situations. I went on to officiate for several years after my college graduation and even got to referee a few college basketball games and some of the biggest high school games in the area. As I look back, I realize that if it were not for my coach, Willie Bell, giving me guidance at a low point in my life, I would have never known about the opportunity to be a referee and would have missed out on so much.

Author's Thankful Thoughts

I appreciate the extra time my coach invested in me and the advice he gave. I am also grateful that I now have the opportunity to guide and counsel others. As time goes on, I become more aware of how guidance from others has helped me throughout my life. It has been such a blessing. Most importantly, though, I am so thankful for God and His guidance every day of my life. Without His leadership, I have no idea where I would be. It is an honor to know that He cares about and loves me enough to be my personal Guide and show me the right paths to take in life.

Go Deeper: Exodus 13:21-22, Psalm 139:8-10, Proverbs 11:14, Isaiah 58:11

Points to consider as we thank God for **GUIDANCE**:

- How many times have you experienced guidance from another person? How often do you guide others?

- Are there any people you need to thank because of the direction they've given you in your life?

- God is your ultimate guide. How can you show your gratitude to Him?

My Thankful Life

_____

_____

_____

_____

_____

_____

_____

_____

_____

_____

_____

_____

_____

_____

_____

My Thankful Thoughts

_____

_____

_____

_____

_____

_____

_____

_____

_____

_____

_____

_____

_____

_____

_____

LAUGHTER

"He will yet fill your mouth with
laughter and your lips with
shouts of joy."
— Job 8:21

I really enjoy a good laugh. I think we all do. Growing up, we were always doing silly things to get a laugh. As a family, humor was just part of the daily routine around our house.

My grandmother was always someone I could count on for a good laugh. Let me give you a little background on my dear "Grandma." My grandmother was a very righteous and spiritual woman. She knew the Lord and how to connect with Him. When I was diagnosed with cancer, I remember my dad saying, "Son, don't worry about anything. Your grandmother is praying for you." I understand what my dad meant. Whenever we stayed at my grandmother's house, she would go to her room at night to pray and read her Bible. When she prayed, she would pray out loud and cry out to the Lord. Her prayers were not quick either. They would go on and on! I am thankful for her prayers.

My grandmother also liked to laugh and enjoyed good humor. One time when my brother and I were visiting her, she came home from church very confused. As we questioned her, she tried to tell us the story about what had happened, but she was laughing so hard she could barely get it out. You see, as she was driving home from church that afternoon, a car pulled up beside her. The teenagers inside were blowing the horn, yelling and carrying on. Well, when my grandmother drove, she always had two hands on the steering wheel, a firm grip, and looked straight ahead no distractions. But they continued to blow the horn, so finally she looked over and there was a boy's backside hanging out of the window of the car. My grandmother did not understand that they were mooning her. She just looked at him and said to herself, Why does that boy have his backside hanging out the window? When she came home and told us the story, we all laughed for hours! My grandmother was firm, bold and funny. I remember the first time I took my wife (then fiancé), Jacqui, to meet her. We were sitting on the couch when I said, "Grandma, this is the lady I'm going to marry. She is a Christian and loves the Lord."

My grandmother paused and said, "Robert, a lot of people say they are Christians, but they really aren't." Jacqui felt like crawling under that couch! Thankfully, she and my grandmother developed a very special relationship over the years, and now we laugh about the day they first met.

Another time, Jacqui and I were going to church with my grandmother. Right before we walked into the sanctuary, she grabbed Jacqui's arm and said, "Buckle up, honey." (My grandmother's church was very charismatic.) Today, we still laugh about her and the way she would do and say things.

My kids left today to visit my parents while they are on Easter break. I pray that they have the same fun time visiting their grandparents as I had visiting mine as a child. I want them to have many memories to look back on and laugh about, too.

Author's Thankful Thoughts

I am thankful for pure laughter. It is indeed good medicine for the heart and soul. I am especially thankful for my grandmother, her sense of humor, and the memories we shared together. Times of laughter are some of the best moments in life. God designed us to enjoy this life He has blessed us with, and being cheerful is one way to do that.

Go Deeper: Psalm 126:2-3, Proverbs 15:13, 15, 30, Proverbs 17:22

Points to consider as we thank God for **LAUGHTER**:

- Do you often experience moments of pure laughter with those around you?

- Do you have cheerful memories that you can thank God for right now?

- Is your heart joyful even when life's circumstances are not the best?

_____

_____

_____

_____

_____

_____

_____

_____

_____

_____

_____

_____

_____

_____

_____

My Thankful Thoughts

_____

_____

_____

_____

_____

_____

_____

_____

_____

_____

_____

_____

_____

_____

_____

PROTECTION

"But the Lord is faithful, and he will
strengthen and protect you. . ."
- 2 Thessalonians 3:3

When I was a kid, we lived across the street from a park. It had a baseball field, a full basketball court, a sandbox, woods, and some great hills for sledding in the snow. There was also a creek, great for catching crawdads! One afternoon, my brother and I were at the park playing basketball. We were having great time playing and enjoying the day until two or three car loads of people showed up to play, as well. They tried to run my brother and me off the court. I said to myself, No, we were here first. They can play on one half of the court, and we can play on the other half. They still tried to tell us to leave.

They were young adults with drivers licenses; we were only 12 or 13. So eventually they did run us off the court, and we went home. When we got home and told our dad what had happened, he was not very happy about it. The park was public, but these guys had driven in from another part of town. This was our neighborhood park. My father felt like we should have at least been able to share the court with them. So he left the house and began to walk to the park. My brothers and I were watching from one of the windows upstairs, trying to see through the trees what was happening. I was a little afraid because there were about 15 to 20 guys that my dad was going to confront by himself. Those weren't very good odds if something happened. But once my dad got there, it was only a matter of seconds before the basketball court cleared and all those guys packed up and left. To this day, I don't know what he said to them. I've never asked. What I do remember is that my dad was willing to stand up for his children even when he was outnumbered. It was this type of behavior that always kept me feeling protected and safe as I grew up.

Author's Thankful Thoughts

I am thankful for the protection my parents provided for me as a child. I am also thankful that now, as a parent, I have the opportunity to protect and stand up for my family. I could never express my gratitude to the Lord for the protection He offers each and every day. It is because of Him that I can feel safe and secure in any situation.

Go Deeper: Deuteronomy 32:10-11, Psalm 5:11-12, Psalm 91, Psalm 125:1-2, Proverbs 18:10, Isaiah 25:4-5, 2 Thessalonians 3:3

Points to consider as we thank God for **PROTECTION**:

- When have you been protected by someone else? Have you shown your gratitude?

- Are you one who protects others and helps them feel safe?

- Consider the ways God offers you His protection on a daily basis.

_____

_____

_____

_____

_____

_____

_____

_____

_____

_____

_____

_____

_____

_____

_____

_____

My Thankful Thoughts

_____

_____

_____

_____

_____

_____

_____

_____

_____

_____

_____

_____

_____

_____

_____

Bible Verses

There are over 160 verses in the Bible that refer to thankfulness, giving thanks, etc. As you probably noticed, before every short story there was a Bible verse related to the subject of that particular story. Our goal is to encourage the readers of this book to "dig deeper" and find verses that pertain to the short stories they write too. Therefore, we thought it would be helpful to list all of the Bible verses that mention the word, thank. Readers can use the list as a reference or guide as they write their stories of thankfulness.

1. Leviticus 7:12
2. Leviticus 7:13
3. Leviticus 7:15
4. Leviticus 22:29
5. Ruth 2:10
6. 1 Samuel 1:18
7. 1 Samuel 25:33
8. 2 Samuel 7:18
9. 2 Samuel 14:9
10. 1 Chronicles 16:4
11. 1 Chronicles 16:7
12. 1 Chronicles 16:8
13. 1 Chronicles 16:34
14. 1 Chronicles 16:35
15. 1 Chronicles 16:41
16. 1 Chronicles 17:16
17. 1 Chronicles 23:30
18. 1 Chronicles 25:3
19. 1 Chronicles 29:13
20. 2 Chronicles 5:13
21. 2 Chronicles 20:21
22. 2 Chronicles 20:26
23. 2 Chronicles 29:31
24. 2 Chronicles 30:22
25. 2 Chronicles 31:2
26. 2 Chronicles 33:16
27. Ezra 3:11
28. Nehemiah 11:17
29. Nehemiah 12:8
30. Nehemiah 12:24
31. Nehemiah 12:27
32. Nehemiah 12:31
33. Nehemiah 12:38
34. Nehemiah 12:40
35. Nehemiah 12:46
36. Psalm 7:17
37. Psalm 26:7
38. Psalm 28:7
39. Psalm 30:12
40. Psalm 35:18
41. Psalm 42:4
42. Psalm 50:14
43. Psalm 50:23
44. Psalm 56:12
45. Psalm 57:9
46. Psalm 69:30
47. Psalm 75:1
48. Psalm 79:13
49. Psalm 92:1
50. Psalm 95:2
51. Psalm 100:1
52. Psalm 100:4
53. Psalm 105:1
54. Psalm 106:1
55. Psalm 106:47
56. Psalm 107:1

57. Psalm 107:22
58. Psalm 108:3
59. Psalm 109:30
60. Psalm 111:1
61. Psalm 116:17
62. Psalm 118:1
63. Psalm 118:19
64. Psalm 118:21
65. Psalm 118:29
66. Psalm 119:7
67. Psalm 119:62
68. Psalm 122:4
69. Psalm 136:1
70. Psalm 136:2
71. Psalm 136:3
72. Psalm 136:4
73. Psalm 136:5
74. Psalm 136:6
75. Psalm 136:7
76. Psalm 136:10
77. Psalm 136:13
78. Psalm 136:16
79. Psalm 136:17
80. Psalm 136:26
81. Psalm 138:1
82. Psalm 138:4
83. Psalm 139:14
84. Psalm 142:7
85. Psalm 145:10

86. Psalm 147:7
87. Proverbs 30:11
88. Ecclesiastes 9:15
89. Isaiah 12:4
90. Isaiah 43:20
91. Isaiah 51:3
92. Jeremiah 5:7
93. Jeremiah 17:26
94. Jeremiah 30:19
95. Jeremiah 33:11
96. Daniel 2:23
97. Daniel 6:10
98. Amos 4:5
99. Matthew 11:25
100. Matthew 15:36
101. Matthew 26:27
102. Mark 8:6
103. Mark 14:23
104. Luke 10:21
105. Luke 17:9
106. Luke 17:16
107. Luke 18:11
108. Luke 22:17
109. Luke 22:19
110. John 6:11
111. John 11:41
112. Acts 13:48
113. Acts 27:35
114. Acts 28:15

115. Romans 1:8
116. Romans 1:21
117. Romans 6:17
118. Romans 7:25
119. Romans 14:6
120. Romans 16:4
121. 1 Corinthians 1:4
122. 1 Corinthians 1:14
123. 1 Corinthians 10:30
124. 1 Corinthians 11:24
125. 1 Corinthians 14:16
126. 1 Corinthians 14:17
127. 1 Corinthians 14:18
128. 1 Corinthians 15:57
129. 2 Corinthians 1:11
130. 2 Corinthians 2:14
131. 2 Corinthians 4:15
132. 2 Corinthians 8:16
133. 2 Corinthians 9:11
134. 2 Corinthians 9:12
135. 2 Corinthians 9:15
136. Ephesians 1:16
137. Ephesians 5:4
138. Ephesians 5:20
139. Philippians 1:3
140. Philippians 4:6
141. Philippians 4:10
142. Colossians 1:3
143. Colossians 1:12

144. Colossians 2:7
145. Colossians 3:15
146. Colossians 3:16
147. Colossians 3:17
148. Colossians 4:2
149. 1 Thessalonians 1:2
150. 1 Thessalonians 2:13
151. 1 Thessalonians 3:9
152. 1 Thessalonians 5:18
153. 2 Thessalonians 1:3
154. 2 Thessalonians 2:13
155. 1 Timothy 1:12
156. 1 Timothy 2:1
157. 1 Timothy 4:3
158. 1 Timothy 4:4
159. 2 Timothy 1:3
160. Philemon 1:4
161. Hebrews 12:28
162. Revelation 4:9
163. Revelation 7:12
164. Revelation 11:17

ADDITIONAL BOOKS BY

THE CORE MEDIA GROUP

Silver Anniversary Edition:
Celebrating 25 Years of Sports & Faith

An inspiring book that tells the faith stories of the most prominent Christian sports figures who have appeared in the pages of *Sports Spectrum* magazine the last 25 years.

Called by some the Christian *Sports Illustrated* because of its design and quality, *Sports Spectrum* has interviewed the superstars in the Big Four (NFL, Major League Baseball, NBA and NHL) as well as stars in speedskating, surfing, skateboarding, rodeo, bull riding, and other sports.

Like the magazine, these stories will inspire you in your faith or cause you to examine your life to see if Christ is a part of it.

Price: $25.00
118 pages

Drive Thru Success:
Finding Success While Waiting in the Drive Thru

Looking to live a successful life? Then take a seat and join the ride in Drive Thru Success, by Robert B. Walker - a successful pro sports agent for more than 20 years who uses the drive thru experience as an illustration for finding true success in life. Each step of the drive thru experience represents a different step for success. Everyone has been through a drive thru, so let's learn from it. Learn about life's choices at the drive thru menu. Learn about patience while sitting in line. Learn about trust while getting your order. Drive Thru Success is a great read for everyone of any age who is searching to achieve success in business, athletics, school, and life. So what are you waiting for? Jump in!

Price: $14.95
106 pages

Life Points:
25 Directives That Will Change the Way You Live

Whether you're a businessperson, parent, student, or athlete, life can be confusing. If you don't have the information you want, it can be frustrating. But if you don't have the direction you need, it can be devastating. Life Points has been written to add the directives needed to set your life on a course of success. Among other things, by implementing the individual directives, you'll learn the importance of: Surrounding yourself with the right people; that personal freedom comes from personal discipline; choosing your battles; living a balanced life; taking chances ... and so much more. By systematically following the book's directives, you will have the motivation, information, and plans to accomplish so much more in your life. Life Points will give you the foundation you need to launch your life in a direction that will be fulfilling, exciting, and successful.

Price: $14.95
106 pages

To order the books above 1•866•821•2971 or visit our website at www.sportsspectrum.com

Training Table:
10 For 10 Sports Devotionals For the Seasons Within the Season

The Core Media Group, Inc., and *Sports Spectrum* magazine present Training Table: 10 for 10 - Sports Devotionals for the Seasons Within the Season, is a devotional book for athletes, coaches and sports fans.

This is a unique tool to further the development and spiritual growth of individuals. Sports analogies can teach valuable truths about life as revealed through the truth of the Bible. Training Table: 10 for 10 provides 10 devotionals for 10 topics that provide a truth or biblical principle to apply to your daily life and sporting life.

Price: $12.95
140 pages

Living the Thankful Life

Living the Thankful Life includes 29 short stories about things for which Robert is thankful. It also includes an area to write your own stories of thanks, which enables you to make it a legacy book for you, your family and others concerning living a thankful life.

Wisdom and Sports
Sports Devotionals and Sports Stories Based on the Book of Proverbs

Verses from all 31 chapters of Proverbs are paired with spiritually encouraging stories of well-known athletes and thought-provoking devotionals. You will be inspired as you read each page of this book written by Robert B. Walker.

Cultivating the godly Athlete:
Our Faith On and Off the Field

COMING 2011

[Coming 2011]

Twenty biblical qualities for the spiritual development of athletes on and off the field. This is an in-depth look at what faith on the field looks like, and how our lives as Christians are to be mirrored in all of our endeavors in life including sports.

S&H: $5.95, Canadian: $9.95(US funds only), $2.00 per additional book.

Make checks payable to: Sports Spectrum, PO Box 2037, Indian Trail, NC 28079

Thank You Cards

Thank those you appreciate most.

1. Cut out this Thank You card on the black line

2. Then score the card in half, where the dotted line is.

3. Write your Thank You note on the inside of the card.

4. Then mail it off.

"The word that is heard perishes, but the letter that is written remains."
- Proverb

THANK YOU

Education Guidance

Help Food Literacy Health

Talents and Gifts Fellowship Holy Spirit Silence Friendship Sanitation

Mentors Discipline Ideas Neighbors

Parenting Family Church

Animals Laughter Home Choices

Love Shelter Technology Protection

Clothes

cut along the black line.

THANK YOU

Education
Guidance
Fellowship
Health
Help
Food
Literacy
Talents
and Gifts
Work
Mentors
Discipline
Parenting
Animals
Family
Love
Laughter
Shelter
Clothes
Technology
Home
Protection
Choices
Church
Neighbors
Ideas
Friendship
Sanitation
Holy
Spirit
Silence

cut along the black line.

THANK YOU

Education
Guidance
Literacy
Food
Help
Health
and Gifts
Fellowship
Talents
Work
Mentors
Discipline
Parenting
Family
Animals
Love
Laughter
Shelter
Clothes
Home
Technology
Protection
Choices
Church
Neighbors
Ideas
Sanitation
Friendship
Silence
Spirit
Holy

cut along the black line.

Education
Guidance
Literacy
Food
Help
Health
Fellowship
and Gifts
Talents
Work
Mentors
Discipline
Parenting
Animals
Family
Holy
Spirit Silence
Sanitation
Friendship
Ideas
Neighbors
Church
THANK
YOU
Home
Love
Laughter
Shelter
Clothes
Technology
Protection
Choices

www.ingramcontent.com/pod-product-compliance
Lightning Source LLC
Chambersburg PA
CBHW052034090426
42739CB00010B/1899